SCHOLAS

25 Fun Word Family Plays

Short, Reproducible Plays That Target and Teach the Top Word Families!

Pamela Chanko

New York · Toronto · London · Auckland · Sydney
Mexico City · New Delhi · Hong Kong · Buenos Aires

Teaching *Resources*

Special thanks to Deborah Schecter,
who was there when I got stuck.
Such a kind and patient editor
can turn a writer's luck!

Cover design by Jason Robinson

Interior design by Sydney Wright

Illustrations by Bari Weissman

ISBN: 978-0-545-10338-1

Contents

Introduction

If you're a teacher of young children, you know how exciting their beginning steps on the road to literacy can be. Emergent readers not only delight in their newfound abilities to decipher written text, but also enjoy playing with words and their sounds; young children have a natural affinity for rhythm and rhyme. Teaching word families capitalizes on this interest, using children's natural enjoyment of word play to its greatest potential: helping them become fluent readers.

Word families are chunks of words that not only rhyme, but also use the same spelling pattern to make the same sound. This sound/symbol reliability increases children's sight word vocabulary exponentially. For example, look at the words *cat, sat, mat, rat, bat,* and *sat.* They share a common word ending, or phonogram, which puts them all in the *-at* word family. Once children learn to read the words *cat, sat,* and *mat,* it becomes far easier for them to read words like *slat, spat, flat, that,* and many more. By teaching children to recognize chunks of words, decoding is made far simpler. And when decoding becomes easier, children have more mental energy to spend on the ultimate goal of literacy: comprehension.

The statistics are amazing but true: nearly 500 primary-grade words can be formed from a small group of word families. This means that children not only build sight vocabulary and decoding skills, but also become more familiar with the way words work—making them better spellers and writers, as well!

Each reproducible play in this collection teaches one of the top word families in an entertaining, engaging context. The interesting plots and charming characters in the plays will draw children's interest and put them in the center of the action! Research shows that all learning—including literacy—is more likely to be retained when children take an active role in that learning.

Reading plays also helps children build fluency by giving them plenty of practice reading aloud, which in turn builds confidence, accuracy, and comprehension. Plus, it gives teachers a natural opportunity for assessment. The plays in this collection are easy to use—no props, costumes, or sets are required. Many of the plays are written in verse, which not only builds phonological awareness by emphasizing the rhyming words, but also helps children get a feel for rhythm and meter. Even the plays written in non-rhyming prose will help children tune in to the musicality of language with devices such as repetition and patterned text.

The plays are also designed to provide you with maximum flexibility in the classroom. You'll find plays that can be used with a variety of groupings, from pairs to

small groups to the whole class. You'll also find roles appropriate for different skill levels, so you can assign parts that provide just the right challenge for each learner.

All you need is a copier and you're ready to give children the combined benefits of word family instruction and rich, meaningful, read-aloud experiences. But perhaps most important of all, you'll find that all of the plays included in *25 Fun Word Family Plays* really are FUN! And the more that young learners associate reading with fun, the more likely they are to develop a love of literacy to last a lifetime!

Connections to the Language Arts Standards

McREL Standards

Mid-continent Research for Education and Learning (McREL), a nationally recognized, nonprofit organization, has compiled and evaluated national and state standards, and proposed what teachers should provide for their K–2 students to grow proficient in language arts, among other curriculum areas. The activities in this book support the following standards:

Uses the general skills and strategies of the reading process:
- Uses mental images based on pictures and print to aid in comprehension of text
- Uses meaning clues (for example, illustrations, title, story structure, story topic) to aid comprehension and make predictions about content (for example, action, events, character's behavior)
- Uses basic elements of phonetic analysis (for example, common letter/sound relationships, beginning and ending consonants, vowel sounds, blends, and word patterns) to decode unknown words
- Uses basic elements of structural analysis (for example, syllables and spelling patterns) to decode unknown words
- Understands level-appropriate sight words and vocabulary
- Reads aloud familiar stories, poems, and passages with fluency and expression (for example, rhythm, flow, meter, intonation, and tempo)

Uses reading skills and strategies to understand and interpret a variety of literary texts:
- Understands a variety of familiar passages and texts (for example, fiction, poems, and rhymes)
- Knows the basic characteristics of familiar genres
- Knows setting, main characters, main events, sequence, narrator, and problems in stories
- Knows the main ideas or theme of a story, drama, or poem

Uses listening and speaking strategies for different purposes:
- Uses different voice level, phrasing, and intonation for different situations
- Recites and responds to familiar stories, poems, and rhymes with patterns

Source: Kendall, J. S. and Marzano, R. J. (2004). *Content knowledge: A compendium of standards and benchmarks for K-12 education*. Aurora, CO: Mid-continent Research for Education and Learning. Online database: http://www.mcrel.org/standards-benchmarks/

Common Core State Standards

The activities in this book also correlate with the English Language Arts standards recommended by the Common Core State Standards Initiative, a state-led effort to establish a single set of clear educational standards whose aim is to provide students with a high-quality education. At the time that this book went to press, these standards were still being finalized. To learn more, go to www.corestandards.org.

 # Using the Plays

Use the following tips and ideas to get the most
out of using the plays in your classroom.

Before Reading

❖ Make a copy of the play for each child.

❖ Preview the play with children by copying it onto transparency film for use on an overhead projector or scan to display on an interactive whiteboard. This way, you can track the print when you first read the play with the group.

❖ Before reading the play, introduce the word family children will be working with. Say the phonogram aloud, point to the letters, and have children repeat the phonogram after you. Explain that in the play, children will see many words that end with the same letters and sounds. You might even help children brainstorm a few words from the word family and predict which might be part of the story.

❖ Assign parts to children according to their reading readiness. You'll find that some parts require more reading than others, and some also contain more repetition than others. You'll also want to consider whether children are ready to read on their own, or would be more comfortable reading along with a group, and assign parts accordingly. You might have a small group of children chorally read the text for one role.

❖ Once children have been assigned roles, provide them with highlighters so they can mark their lines. When children are ready to read the play aloud, the highlighting will allow them to find their parts quickly and easily.

During Reading

❖ The first time you read each play, you may want to read all of the text aloud yourself. This will not only familiarize children with the language, but also give them a preview of the characters and plot.

❖ Read the play straight through the first time, focusing on expression and rhythm. On the second reading, invite children to pay special attention to words from the word family. Each time they see or hear a word family word, they can signal by raising their hands.

❖ Children's readings of the plays can take place in a variety of ways: For instance, children can do an informal reading by sitting in a circle, each child reading his or her part aloud. You might also have children do a more "formal" Reader's Theater performance, having them stand in front of the room and read the play aloud to the class audience. The class can simply watch the performance, or they might like to follow along using their own copies of the play.

25 Fun Word Family Plays © 2011 by Pamela Chanko, Scholastic Teaching Resources

❖ If using the plays with small groups, consider giving each group a different play to practice simultaneously as you circulate, providing assistance as needed. Then, when groups are ready, they can take turns performing their plays for the class.

❖ While the plays require no costumes or props, you might consider using puppets with children who may be uncomfortable performing in front of a group. Simple stick puppets can give children just the distance they need to ease any "stage fright" they may feel. You can even make a simple puppet theater by covering a small table with a cloth and having children kneel behind it, holding up the puppets as they read.

After Reading

❖ Create an instant listening center by making a recording of children's readings. Place the recording in the center along with copies of the play and have children follow along with their own performance!

❖ Challenge children to circle each word they find that belongs to the featured word family. This can also provide you with an easy way to assess learning.

❖ Forge home-school connections by sending children home with a copy of the play to read with family members. You might even include a short note inviting families to do a quick, related activity with their child. For instance, family members might go on a scavenger hunt with their child, finding as many words from the target word family as they can in that day's newspaper.

FUN Word Family Activities

Use these quick and easy hands-on activities and games
to give children even more practice—and fun—with word families!

Word Family Relay

In this active game, children race to form words using common endings.

1. Divide the class into two equal teams. Write the same target phonogram on opposite sides of the chalk- or whiteboard, writing the word ending once for each team member. (For example, to practice the *-op* family with two teams of eight, you would write *op* eight times in a column on each side of the board.)

2. Have each team line up in front of their side of the board and give the first child in each line a piece of chalk (or whiteboard pen). When you say, "Go," that child goes to the board and adds a letter or letters to the first phonogram to form a word. (In this case, a child might add an *m* to the first *op* to form *mop*.) The next player in line then adds letters to form a new word for the list. Teams should not repeat words on their own list, nor peek at the other team's words!

3. Play continues until each team has completed their word list. The team that completes their list first wins the game. Compare word lists. Did teams form mostly the same words, or is each team's list different?

Sprout-a-Word File Folder Game

This easy-to-make game is perfect for learning-center fun!

1. On the inside of a file folder, draw four flowers (two on each side); create daisy-like flowers with a round center and four petals each. Label the center circle of each flower with a phonogram (for example, *-an*, *-ug*, *-ell*, and *-ip*).

2. Next, cut 16 "petals" from cardstock, sizing them to fit on top of the petals on the folder flowers. Write a word on each petal, writing four words for each phonogram you chose. (In this case, you might write *man*, *can*, *van pan*; *bug*, *rug*, *tug*, *dug*; *tell*, *smell*, *bell*, *well*; and *slip*, *rip*, *tip*, *clip*.)

3. Attach a piece of Velcro to each petal on the folder flowers, and another piece to the back of each cardstock petal. (Make sure to use opposite sides of the Velcro so the petals will attach to the folder flowers).

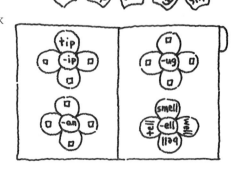

4. Finally, staple an envelope to the back of the folder to store the petals when not in use. To play, children take turns placing a petal word on the flower labeled with the corresponding word family. Play continues until all of the flowers are filled.

8

Join the Word Family Train!

Use this fun transition activity to gather children for circle time—or any time!

1. Begin a conga-style line by snaking around the room and announcing a word family. For example, you might say, "Join the word family train! We're carrying words that end with -at!" Stop in front of a child and encourage him or her to name an -at word (such as mat), then join the line by placing his or hands on your waist.

2. Continue snaking around the room, stopping in front of each child and having him or her say another word from the word family before joining the back of the "train." Once all children have gotten "aboard," you can lead the line over to the circle-time rug, or wherever you're doing the next activity.

Word Family Freeze 'n' Go

This game improves listening skills while keeping children moving!

1. Clear an open area and have children form a horizontal line against a wall, or have them stand on a starting line that you've marked with masking tape. Stand at a distance, facing the group, and announce a target phonogram (for instance, -est). Explain to children that you will be calling out some words, and it is their job to move forward until they tag you. The catch? Children may only move on -est words! If they hear a word that does not end with -est, they must freeze in place.

2. Begin calling out words (such as nest, best, pest) as children move forward, and then randomly insert a word from a different family (such as snake). Anyone caught moving on that word must return to the starting line and begin again. Continue calling out words as children freeze and go. The first child to reach you wins and gets to be the next word-caller. (If children have trouble calling words spontaneously, you might give callers a word list or word cards to read from.)

What Would Jack Pack?

In this game, children pack a suitcase for a word family vacation!

1. Seat children in a circle for this variation on a popular memory game. Choose a word family that includes a proper name, such as Jack, Jan, Pat, or Bill. Then begin the game by saying, for example: "Pat is packing a suitcase and she's bringing a _____." Fill the blank with another word from the family, for instance, cat.

2. The child to your left repeats the sentence and adds another item from the word family, for example, "Pat is packing a suitcase and she's bringing a cat and a hat." Continue around the circle, having each child repeat the previous items and add a new one. Play until the chain breaks—either because you run out of words, or the list gets too long to remember! Then the last child to correctly complete the sentence chain gets to start a new suitcase with a new name.

Word Family Flip Books

Use everyday classroom supplies to create fun, word-building flip books!

1. You can create these interactive books yourself, or have children help you make them. For each book, you will need a 4- by 6-inch index card and a thin stack of standard 3- by 3-inch sticky notes. Positioning the card horizontally, attach the sticky notes to the left side. Place one or two staples at the top of the sticky note stack to make sure the "pages" stay in place.

2. To fill in the book, write a word ending on the index card next to the sticky note stack. Then, write a different initial consonant, blend, or digraph on each sticky note page to form a word with the target phonogram. For instance, if you've written the word ending -*ight* on the card, you might write the following letters on each page: *l, n, r, s, br, fl*, and so on.

3. To use the books, children simply flip back each page and read the new word that appears (in this case, *light, night, right, sight, bright*, and *flight*). Children can make a flip book for each word family they learn and store them all in a file card box.

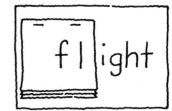

Who's in My Family?

Have a word family reunion right in your classroom!

1. In advance, create sets of word cards for different phonograms, about four to five words per set. (For example, one set of cards might have the words *bake, cake, snake, lake*, and *take*.) Create enough cards for each child to get one, making sure that each child will belong to a small group. Punch a hole in the top of each card and string with yarn to make a necklace.

2. Give each child a necklace and have children walk around the room with their words facing out. When they spot a child with a word from the same family, they begin traveling together to look for other group members. Continue until each family has been "reunited"!

3. Once children have found their groups, give each group a sentence strip and challenge groups to write a silly sentence containing all of their words. (For example, "Let's bake a cake to take to the snake by the lake.") Let groups take turns sharing their words and sentences with the class.

25 Fun Word Family Plays © 2011 by Pamela Chanko, Scholastic Teaching Resources

Zack's Shack

Characters

Narrator	Mole	Chicken	Kangaroo
Zack	Deer	Wolf	Jack

Narrator: Zack was a black sheep.
He lived all alone in a shack.

Zack: It is very lonely in my shack.
I need a friend
to come live with me.

Narrator: First, Zack saw Mole.

Mole: I will live in your shack, Zack.
I can dig a track for you.

Zack: I do not need a track for my shack.

Narrator: Then Zack saw Deer.

Deer: I will live in your shack, Zack.
You can use my horns
for a hat rack.

Zack: I do not need a hat rack
in my shack.

Narrator: Then Zack saw Chicken.

Chicken: I will live in your shack, Zack.
You can crack my eggs
for a snack.

Zack: I do not need
a snack in my shack.

Narrator: Next, Zack saw Wolf.

Wolf: I will live in your shack, Zack.
I can bring my whole pack with me.

Zack: I do not need
a wolf pack in my shack.

Narrator: Next, Zack saw Kangaroo.

Kangaroo: I will live in your shack, Zack.
I will hold your mail in my sack.

Zack: I do not need a mail sack
in my shack.

Narrator: Then Zack saw Jack.
Jack was a black duck.

Jack: I will live in your shack, Zack.
But all I can do is quack.

Zack: That is just what I need
in my shack!
It is too quiet here all by myself.

Narrator: Zack was not lonely
with Jack in his shack.
When Zack talked to Jack,
Jack would always quack back!

The End

✦✦✦✦✦✦✦

25 Fun Word Family Plays © 2011 by Pamela Chanko, Scholastic Teaching Resources

On the Trail With Snail and Quail

Characters

Narrator   Snail
Quail   Animals

Narrator: This is the story of Snail and Quail.
They lived in the forest near a trail.

Quail: Hello.
Where are you going, Snail?

Snail: I'm going hiking up the trail.

Quail: You are?
You move so slowly, Snail!

Snail: I hike every day without fail.
I hike through rain.
I hike through hail.

Quail: I'll bet I can hike faster, Snail.

Snail: Really?
I will race you, Quail.

Narrator: All of the animals came to the trail.
They came to watch Quail race Snail.

Animals: Ready, set, go!
Go, Quail! Go, Snail!

Narrator: Slowly, Snail went up the trail.
Quail raced far ahead of Snail.

13

Quail: Snail's so slow, I cannot fail.
I will stop to read my mail.

Animals: Look at Snail hike up the trail!

Quail: Now I'll stop to clean my tail.

Animals: Snail's still going up the trail!

Quail: I still have time.
I'll pick some flowers.
I'll fill my pail.

Animals: Snail's still going.
Watch out, Quail!

Narrator: But Snail had reached
the end of the trail.
When Quail saw him,
he began to wail:

Quail: I can't believe you beat me, Snail!

Snail: Maybe you need practice, Quail.
Meet me tomorrow.
We'll hike the trail.
Be there at ten o'clock on the nail!

Narrator: And ever since then, without fail
they hike every day—
even through rain, even through hail!
So if you go hiking on the trail,
look out—you might see Snail and Quail!

The End

✦✦✦✦✦✦✦

25 Fun Word Family Plays © 2011 by Pamela Chanko, Scholastic Teaching Resources

Wake Up, Jake!

Characters
Blake	Mom
Jake	Dad

Blake: Jake is still asleep.
Wake up, Jake!
Mom says we have
leaves to rake.

Jake: Zzzzzzz.

Blake: Jake, it's morning.
Wake up, Jake!
Dad says we have
beds to make.

Jake: Zzzzzzz.

Blake: It's time for chores.
Wake up, Jake!
We have to clean the cage
of our pet snake.

Jake: Zzzzzzz.

Blake: Please stop snoring.
Wake up, Jake!
I need your help,
for goodness' sake!

Jake: Zzzzzzz.

Blake: Can't you hear me?
Wake up, Jake!
How much longer will this take?

Mom: Good morning.
What's the matter, Blake?

Blake: I tried, but I can't wake up Jake!

Mom: I'll wake him up.
He just needs a little shake.

Jake: Zzzzzzz.

Dad: Good morning.
What is wrong with Jake?

Mom: He's fast asleep.
He will not wake.

Jake: Zzzzzzz.

Blake: We have chores to do.
That snore sounds fake.
He doesn't want to help me rake!

Dad: Mom and I will help you, Blake.

Mom: And after chores, we'll have some cake.

Jake: What kind of cake will we bake?

Dad: We thought that you were sleeping, Jake.

Jake: Not anymore—
there's cake to make!

The End

✦ ✦ ✦ ✦ ✦ ✦ ✦

25 Fun Word Family Plays © 2011 by Pamela Chanko, Scholastic Teaching Resources

Stan, the Fix-It Man

Characters

Nan   Jan
Dan   Stan

Nan: I am hot.
Who broke my fan?

Dan: It wasn't me.
You should call Stan.

Nan: Who is Stan?

Dan: Stan is the fix-it man!
If Stan can't fix it,
no one can.

Jan: Hey!
Who broke my best toy van?
Was it Dan or Nan?

Dan and Nan: It wasn't us.
You should call Stan.

Jan: Who is Stan?

Dan and Nan: Stan is the fix-it man!
If Stan can't fix it,
no one can.

25 Fun Word Family Plays © 2011 by Pamela Chanko, Scholastic Teaching Resources

Dan: Look!
The handle broke off my pan!
Who broke it?

Jan and Nan: It wasn't us, Dan.
Why don't you call Stan?

Dan: Oh, no!
Who spilled this raisin bran?

Nan: There's a trail of bran.
Let's follow it, Jan.

Jan: I see something black and tan.

Nan, Jan, and Dan: Oh! It is our ferret, Fran!
She chewed the box of raisin bran!

Nan: Look!
She has the cord
from my fan!

Jan: She took the wheels
off my toy van!

Dan: And there's the handle
from my pan!

Jan and Nan: She just ran off!
Come back, Fran!
We still love you!
Catch her, Dan!

Dan: There she is! And look—
she brought back Stan!

25 Fun Word Family Plays © 2011 by Pamela Chanko, Scholastic Teaching Resources

Stan: Did someone need
a fix-it man?

Nan, Jan, and Dan: Yes! We have a broken fan.
We also have this van and pan.
Can you fix them?

Stan: Yes, I can!

All: If Stan can't fix it,
no one can!

The End

Thank You, Hank!

Characters

Mom	Sis
Hank	Baby Frank
Dad	

Mom: The fish tank is dirty.
Will you clean it, Hank?

Hank: Sure.

Mom: Thank you, Hank!

Dad: This plank in the floor is loose.
Will you fix it, Hank?

Hank: Sure.

Dad: Thank you, Hank!

Sis: My favorite shirt shrank.
Will you stretch it, Hank?

Hank: Sure.

Sis: Thank you, Hank!

Mom: We drank all the milk.
Will you get more, Hank?

Hank: Sure.

25 Fun Word Family Plays © 2011 by
Pamela Chanko, Scholastic Teaching Resources

Mom: Thank you, Hank!

Dad: I don't have time to go to the bank.
Will you go for me, Hank?

Hank: Sure.

Dad: Thank you, Hank!

Sis: I can't write my book report.
My mind is blank.
Will you help me, Hank?

Hank: Sure.

Sis: Thank you, Hank!

Baby Frank: Waaaaaah! Waaaaaah!

Hank: Don't cry, Baby Frank.
I've got you.
Shhhhh . . . there, there.
That's better.

Baby Frank: Thank you, Hank!

Mom: Was that Baby Frank?

Dad: Yes! He said his first words!

Sis: And he said them to *you*, Hank!

Hank: Yes, he did.
Thank you, Baby Frank!

The End

♦♦♦♦♦♦♦

25 Fun Word Family Plays © 2011 by Pamela Chanko, Scholastic Teaching Resources

Tippy Turtle Learns to Tap

Characters

Penny Penguin   Harry Horse
Tippy Turtle   Ricky Rabbit
Susan Swan   Mrs. Moo-Cow

Penny Penguin: Tap, tap, tap.
Tappety-tappety-tap!

Tippy Turtle: I wish I could
tap dance like Penny.

Susan Swan: It takes practice.
It isn't a snap!

Penny Penguin: Every week, I strap on
my tap shoes
and go to tap class.
Try it!

Tippy Turtle: I don't have any talent—
not a scrap!

Harry Horse: You don't know that, old chap.

Ricky Rabbit: Harry's right.
You yap about tap,
but you never try!

22

25 Fun Word Family Plays © 2011 by
Pamela Chanko, Scholastic Teaching Resources

Penny Penguin: Let's go, Tippy!
Get your cap.

Tippy Turtle: Now?
I was about to take a nap.

**Susan Swan,
Harry Horse,
and Ricky Rabbit:** Go on, Tippy!
It's not a trap!

Penny Penguin: Here we are!
Mrs. Moo-Cow, this is Tippy.

Mrs. Moo-Cow: Strap on these tap shoes, Tippy!
Five, six, seven, eight!
Tap, tap, tap!
Tap, slap, snap!

**Penny Penguin
and Other Animals:** Tap, tap, tap!
Tap, slap, snap!

Tippy Turtle: Flip, flap, flap!
Flop, flip, flap!
Oh, no!
I'm all over the map!

Mrs. Moo-Cow: Keep trying!
Tappety-tappety, tap!

Tippy Turtle: Tappety-flappety, flap!

Mrs. Moo-Cow: That's better!
Rap, snap, tappety-tap!

Tippy Turtle: Rap, snap, tappety-tap!

**Mrs. Moo-Cow,
Penny Penguin,
and Other Animals:** Clap, clap, clap, clap,
clap, clap, clap, clap!

Tippy Turtle: Clap, clap . . . what was that?

Penny Penguin: That was everyone clapping, Tippy!
You did it!

Tippy Turtle: You were all clapping for me?
Snappety-snap!
I am learning to tap!

The End

25 Fun Word Family Plays © 2011 by Pamela Chanko, Scholastic Teaching Resources

Drat That Cat!

Nat: Come here, Pat.
Look at my hat.

Pat: What's wrong with it?

Nat: My hat is flat!
Your cat sat on it.
Drat that cat!

Pat: My cat did not sit on your hat.
She wouldn't do a thing like that.

Nat: What about my baseball bat?
Your cat chewed on it.
Drat that cat!

Pat: My cat did not chew on your bat.
She wouldn't do a thing like that.

Nat: Look at that mat.
It's got a splat.
That was your cat.
Admit it, Pat!
Who else would do a thing like that?

Pat: I don't know, but not my cat.

25

Nat: She hissed at me.
She also spat.
She doesn't go when I say, "Scat!"
She never listens.
Drat that . . . RAT!

Pat: I know that you don't like her, Nat.
But please don't call my cat a rat!

Nat: No, I mean it!
Look at that!
A big fat rat came through that slat!
Oh, my gosh!
Do something, Pat!

Pat: I'm sorry, I can't help you, Nat.
I don't know how to scare a rat.
But I wonder . . .
who might be able to do a thing like that?

Nat: Drat! Your cat!
Okay, you win—
Go ahead and call her, Pat.

Pat: Here she comes!
There goes the rat!
Now, please say you're sorry, Nat.

Nat: You were right.
I'm sorry, Pat.

Pat: Don't tell me—tell my cat!

The End

✦✦✦✦✦✦✦

25 Fun Word Family Plays © 2011 by Pamela Chanko, Scholastic Teaching Resources

Nate and Tate Are Late

Characters

Nate   Kate
Tate   Friends

Nate: Tate, let's go.
We have a date with Kate.

Tate: We do? I forgot.
I'm so busy!
I'll be ready to go soon.

Nate: Hurry up, Tate.
I don't want to be late.

Tate: We'll go after I grate this cheese.

Nate: Hurry up, Tate.
It's getting late.

Tate: We'll go after I eat
this plate of tater tots.

Nate: Hurry up, Tate.
We might be late!

Tate: We'll go after I fix my roller skate.

Nate: Hurry up, Tate!
We're running late!

Tate: We'll go after I paint the front gate.

Nate: Hurry up, Tate!
It's really late!

Tate: We'll go after I move this crate.

Nate: We'll never go at this rate!
I mean it, Tate!
We can't be late!

Tate: Okay, Nate!
We'll go right now.
Why are you so upset?
Kate won't hate us if we're late!

Nate: It's very important to be on time today.

Tate: Why? What's so special about today?

Nate: I can't believe you don't know
what date it is!

Tate: Sorry, Nate.
Well, here we are.

Kate: Nate and Tate!
You're just in time!

Friends: SURPRISE!
HAPPY BIRTHDAY, TATE!

Tate: It's my birthday?
I was so busy, I forgot the date!

Kate: You always do.
That's why we can surprise you
every year!

Nate: And every year, we're almost late!

Tate: But we always make it—
thanks to Nate!

The End

✦✦✦✦✦✦✦

25 Fun Word Family Plays © 2011 by Pamela Chanko, Scholastic Teaching Resources

Ray, the Jay

Characters

Mama Jay	Fay Jay	May Jay
Papa Jay	Kay Jay	Ray Jay

Mama Jay: Papa Jay, let's build a nest.
I have four eggs to lay.

Papa Jay: Okay, your nest is ready.
It is made of clay and hay.

Mama Jay: Now my eggs are warm.
They may hatch this very day.

Papa Jay: Look!
The eggs are cracking.
Baby birds are on the way.

Mama Jay: Yay!
Let's give them names that rhyme.
Fay, Kay, May, and Ray.

Papa Jay: Hello, my baby jay-birds.
What do you have to say?

Fay Jay: Tweet!
I want to leave the nest.
I want to fly and play.

Kay Jay: Tweet!
That sounds like fun.
I want to go with Fay.

May Jay: Tweet!
I want to come along!
I'll go with Fay and Kay.

Ray Jay: This nest is nice and warm.
You can fly.
I think I'll stay.

Mama Jay: But Ray, you are a jay-bird.
Jay-birds tweet and fly all day.

Ray Jay: If you say so, I will tweet.
But I will not fly—no way!

Fay Jay: Ray is just a scaredy-cat!

Kay Jay: No, he's a scaredy-jay!

May Jay: Look!
That gray cat isn't scared.
He's coming right this way!

Ray Jay: Everybody flap your wings!

Papa Jay: Yes! Let's follow Ray!

Fay, Kay, and May Jay: Phew! We made it.
Ray, you saved the day!

Ray Jay: Tweet, tweet!
I like flying!
I am not a scaredy-jay!

All: Hooray!

The End

25 Fun Word Family Plays © 2011 by Pamela Chanko, Scholastic Teaching Resources

Go to Sleep, Sheep

Characters

Mother Sheep   Sister Sheep
Brother Sheep   Baby Sheep
Father Sheep

Mother Sheep: It's late.
It's time for bed.
Come along, my little sheep.
I'll tuck you in
and say goodnight.
Then you must go to sleep.

Brother Sheep: Don't you hear those crickets?
Listen to them cheep!
The noise is very loud.
I cannot go to sleep.

Father Sheep: Tiny crickets cannot keep
a sheep from going to sleep.

Sister Sheep: The baby birds are still awake.
I can hear them peep.
I want to stay up, too.
I cannot go to sleep.

Mother Sheep: Baby birds cannot keep
a sheep from going to sleep.

25 Fun Word Family Plays © 2011 by Pamela Chanko, Scholastic Teaching Resources

Brother Sheep: Cars and jeeps are passing.
I think I heard one beep.
Can't we take a drive?
I cannot go to sleep.

Father Sheep: A car or jeep cannot keep
a sheep from going to sleep!

Mother Sheep: Father Sheep is right.
Just look at Baby Sheep!
He doesn't hear these sounds.
His sleep is always deep.

Baby Sheep: I do hear all those sounds.
I hear the crickets cheep.
I hear the peep of every bird
and all the cars and
jeeps that beep.

Sister Sheep: Don't the noises
keep you up?

Baby Sheep: No, I just count sheep!

The End

25 Fun Word Family Plays © 2011 by Pamela Chanko, Scholastic Teaching Resources

Please Don't Yell, Nell!

Characters

Dell	Ms. Pell
Nell	Ariell
Tyrell	

Dell: I went to the beach this weekend.
Look at the shell I found.

Nell: THAT'S A NICE SHELL, DELL!

Dell: Nell, please don't yell!

Tyrell: I shouldn't have come to school.
I have a cold.
I can't smell anything.

Nell: I'M SORRY YOU'RE NOT WELL, TYRELL!

Tyrell: Nell, please don't yell!

Ms. Pell: Children, that was the bell.
Recess is over.
It's time for spelling.
Please go inside.

Nell: I LIKE TO SPELL, MS. PELL!

Ms. Pell: Nell, please don't yell!

Ariell: We're coming, Ms. Pell!
Wait a minute, you guys.

Tyrell: What is it, Ariell?

Ariell: Look what I brought
for show-and-tell.

Dell: It's your pet bunny, Clarabell!

Ariell: Oh no! She got out of her cage!
She's running away! Clarabell!

Tyrell: Did she smell a dog or cat?

Dell: Hurry! She's going near the well!

Ariell: Oh no! She almost fell in!
Clarabell!
Why won't she stop?
She always comes when I call her.

Tyrell: Maybe she can't hear you.

Ariell: Help me, Nell!
Please, just yell!

Nell: CLARABELL!

Dell: She heard you!
Here she comes!

Ariell: Give a yell for Nell!
She saved Clarabell!

Ariell, Dell, and Tyrell: HOORAY FOR NELL!
WE THINK YOUR YELL IS SWELL!

The End

✦✦✦✦✦✦✦

25 Fun Word Family Plays © 2011 by Pamela Chanko, Scholastic Teaching Resources

The Best Pest Contest

-est

Characters

Ant	Cricket
Fly	Caterpillar
Bee	Ladybug
Hornet	

Ant: I am just a little ant.
But I can be a pest!
I am good at spoiling picnics—
much better than the rest!

Fly: You can spoil a picnic.
That does not make you the best.
Flies can buzz in people's ears—
now that is being a pest!

Bee: You buzz and bother people,
but can you pass this test?
I'm a bee. I buzz and sting!
That's what makes me best.

Hornet: You can sting, but so can I.
That doesn't make you best.
People run away each time
they see a hornet's nest!

35

25 Fun Word Family Plays © 2011 by Pamela Chanko, Scholastic Teaching Resources

Cricket: I do not sting people.
I just keep them from their rest.
I'm a cricket, and I'm loud!
I have the best chirp in the West!

Caterpillar: Listen, everybody.
I must get this off my chest.
I am just a caterpillar,
and I know I'm not the best!
I don't do very much.
How can I be a better pest?

Ladybug: Oh, little Caterpillar,
You are not like all the rest!
Don't you see? You're different.
You're not meant to be a pest.
Soon, you'll spin a home
where you'll go to take a rest.
You'll come out as a butterfly . . .

All: . . . and *that* will be the BEST!

The End

25 Fun Word Family Plays © 2011 by Pamela Chanko, Scholastic Teaching Resources

Nick Gets Sick

Characters

Nick	Uncle Dick
Aunt Chick	Rick

Nick: I must stay in bed today.
I'm feeling very sick.

Aunt Chick: Tell me, does your head hurt?

Nick: Yes, it feels as heavy as a brick!

Uncle Dick: What else?

Nick: My hands are so weak,
I cannot flick my wrist!
My throat is also sore,
and my tongue feels very thick.

Uncle Dick: Why don't you rest
and watch a movie?

Nick: Yes! An action move is my pick.

Rick: But action movies
are too noisy,
if your head feels
as heavy as a brick!

Nick: Fine. I'll just watch TV, then.
May I please have the remote, Aunt Chick?

Rick: But how can you use the buttons?
You are much too weak to click!

Aunt Chick: Would some ice cream
help your throat?

Nick: Yes, I'd love to have a lick!

Rick: But how can you lick ice cream.
if your tongue feels very thick?

Aunt Chick: I am getting worried.
Let's call the doctor, quick!

Nick: I don't need a doctor!
They use needles and they stick!

Uncle Dick: Don't be scared. It's not that bad.
It's just a tiny prick.

Nick: No, wait! I feel all better!

Rick: That's amazing!
What a trick!

Nick: Okay, I admit it.
I wasn't really sick.

**Aunt Chick
and
Uncle Dick:** Good!
We were about to go for ice cream.

Rick: And now you can join us, Nick!

The End

✦✦✦✦✦✦

25 Fun Word Family Plays © 2011 by Pamela Chanko, Scholastic Teaching Resources

Little Lion's Nightlight

Characters

Big Lion	Big Tiger
Little Lion	Little Tiger

(At Little Lion's house)

Big Lion: Come, Little Lion!
It's time for your first sleepover!

Little Lion: What if I can't sleep at night?

Big Lion: It will be all right, Little Lion.
That won't happen.

Little Lion: But it might.
What if Little Tiger wants to fight?

Big Lion: It will be all right, Little Lion.
That won't happen.

Little Lion: But it might.
What if my pajamas are too tight?

Big Lion: It will be all right, Little Lion.
That won't happen.

Little Lion: But it might.

Big Lion: Everything will be all right, Little Lion!
What are you so afraid of?

Little Lion: I'm afraid of the dark!

Big Lion: Ask Big Tiger to turn on a nightlight.

Little Lion: But I'm a lion! I should be brave.
I shouldn't need a nightlight.
Little Tiger might laugh.

Big Lion: But he might not.

(Later, at Little Tiger's house)

Big Tiger: It is time for bed now.
I'll turn on your nightlight, Little Tiger.

Little Lion: You use a nightlight? Why?

Little Tiger: If I tell you, you might laugh.

Little Lion: But I might not.

Little Tiger: The dark gives me a fright.
Do you mind the light?
Is it too bright?

Little Lion: Oh, no, Little Tiger.
That nightlight is just right!
Good night!

Little Tiger: Good night!

The End

✦✦✦✦✦✦✦

25 Fun Word Family Plays © 2011 by Pamela Chanko, Scholastic Teaching Resources

Jill and Bill

Characters

Jill   Bill

Jill: I'm Jill.
My best friend is Bill.

Bill: I'm Bill.
My best friend is Jill.

Jill and Bill: We don't agree on most things.
But we like each other still!

Bill: It is very cold today.
Do you feel the chill?

Jill: I do not feel a chill.
I do not feel it, Bill.

Bill: You see? We don't agree.
I guess we never will!

Jill: These pickles are yummy.
Do you like the taste of dill?

Bill: I do not like the taste of dill.
I do not like it, Jill.

Jill: You see? We don't agree.
I guess we never will!

Bill: Maybe we should take a hike.
I'd like to climb that hill.

Jill: I do not want to hike that hill.
I do not want to, Bill.

Bill: You see? We don't agree.
I guess we never will!

Jill: Let's see a scary movie.
Now that would be a thrill!

Bill: Scary movies don't thrill me.
I do not like them, Jill.

Jill: You see? We don't agree.
I guess we never will!

Bill: It's time to make our lunch.
We can cook it on the grill.

Jill: I cannot use the grill.
I do not have that skill!

Bill: What can we do together?
We have a day to fill!

Jill: Let's just talk.
That's what friends do.

Bill: Yes!
We're best friends still.

Jill and Bill: That's one thing we agree on—
and I guess we always will!

The End

✦ ✦ ✦ ✦ ✦ ✦

25 Fun Word Family Plays © 2011 by Pamela Chanko, Scholastic Teaching Resources

The King Hears a Ping

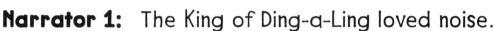

Characters

Narrator 1	Prince
Narrator 2	Princess
King	

Narrator 1: The King of Ding-a-Ling loved noise.
Nothing was loud enough for him.

Narrator 2: When the phone would ring,
the king would shout:

King: Louder! I cannot hear a thing!

Narrator 1: When the birds would sing,
the king would shout:

King: Louder! I cannot hear a thing!

Narrator 2: When the bells would ring,
the king would shout:

King: Louder! I cannot hear a thing!

Narrator 1: The Prince of Ding-a-Ling
hated the noise.

Prince: Ring! Ding! Bing! Zing!
Bring me some earplugs!
My ears sting!

Narrator 2: That spring, a princess came to visit.

Princess: I am the Princess of Ping.
Why is it so noisy here?

King: What? I cannot hear a thing!

Prince: Nothing is loud enough for the king.
But this town makes my ears ring!

Princess: I have an idea.
I will bring the king
to the town of Ping.

Narrator 1: The town of Ping
was not like Ding-a-Ling.
It was quiet.

King: I cannot hear phones ring.
I cannot hear bells ding.

Princess: Shhh. Listen.

King: Oh! What was that tiny ping?

Princess: You heard a pin drop!

King: But in Ding-a-Ling,
I cannot hear a thing!

Princess: That's because it's too noisy there!
You can hear more when
you listen to one thing at a time.

25 Fun Word Family Plays © 2011 by Pamela Chanko, Scholastic Teaching Resources

King: You're right!
I can hear a gate swing!
I can hear a bird flapping its wing!

Narrator 2: The king gave an order:

King: From this day on,
it will be quiet in Ding-a-Ling!

Narrator 1: In Ding-a-Ling, birds still sing.
Phones still ring. Bells still ding.

Prince: But not all at once,
so my ears don't sting!

King and Prince: Thank you, Princess of Ping!
You saved the town of Ding-a-Ling!

The End

25 Fun Word Family Plays © 2011 by Pamela Chanko, Scholastic Teaching Resources

Think Pink!

Characters

Narrator	Blue Bird
Pinky Pig	Yellow Dog
Brown Cow	Orange Cat

Narrator: Pinky Pig just loved to think of things that are the color pink.

Pinky Pig: Bubble gum is nice, I think. And lemonade is good to drink, but only lemonade that is pink!

Narrator: In fact, if something wasn't pink, Pinky Pig would make a stink!

Brown Cow: Let's go to the skating rink.

Pinky Pig: No. The ice rink is not pink.

Blue Bird: Let's take a bath in the kitchen sink.

Pinky Pig: No. The kitchen sink is not pink.

Yellow Dog: Let's build a tower with blocks that link.

Pinky Pig: No. The blocks that link are not pink.

Orange Cat: Let's play with dolls.
They have eyes that blink.

Pinky Pig: No.
Even if their eyes do blink,
I do not like them—
they are not pink.

Narrator: Pinky made her friends' hearts sink.
But then Blue Bird said with a wink:

Blue Bird: I've got it!
Let's make Pinky think
that everything she sees is pink!

Narrator: They solved the problem in a blink.
Can you guess how?
What do you think?

**Brown Cow,
Blue Bird,
Yellow Dog,
and Orange Cat:** We got her eyeglasses
that are tinted pink!

Pinky Pig: Through my rosy glasses,
the whole world looks pink.
And that makes the world look
much better, I think!

The End

✦ ✦ ✦ ✦ ✦ ✦

25 Fun Word Family Plays © 2011 by Pamela Chanko, Scholastic Teaching Resources

Kim and Kip Take a Dip

Characters
Kip   Kim

(In Kim's room)

Kip: It's very hot today!
Do you want to take a dip?

Kim: I can't go to the pool.
I'm very busy, Kip.

Kip: Please come, big sister!
You can teach me how
to do a back flip!
We can get there very fast.
We can run or we can skip!

Kim: I leave for camp tomorrow.
I'm packing for my trip.
I have many things to do,
and nothing I can skip.

Kip: If you take me,
I will let you read
my favorite comic strip.

Kim: Oh, no, my suitcase won't close.
The zipper will not zip!

Kip: If you take me,
I will let you have
my lemonade to sip.

25 Fun Word Family Plays © 2011 by
Pamela Chanko, Scholastic Teaching Resources

Kim: Did I forget my hair brush?
Where's my favorite clip?

Kip: If you take me,
I will let you sail
my favorite toy ship.

Kim: Kip, I can't right now!
My suitcase will not shut,
and now it's starting to rip!

Kip: Kim, it's hot!
Your lip is sweating.
It's starting to drip!
You need to take a break.
You need to get a grip!

Kim: Maybe you are right.

Kip: Let me give you a tip.
Take a dip! Cool off!

Kim: Okay, let's go together, Kip.

(At the pool)

Both: SPLASH!

Kim: This feels great, little brother!
I'll miss you on my trip.

Kip: When I'm older, I can go to camp.

Kim: And every day, we'll take a dip!

The End

25 Fun Word Family Plays © 2011 by Pamela Chanko, Scholastic Teaching Resources

Knock, Knock!

Characters

Mail Carrier	Neighbor	Clockmaker
Voice	Painter	Mr. Brock

Mail Carrier: Knock, knock!

Voice: Who's there?

Mail Carrier: I have your mail, Mr. Brock!

Neighbor: Knock, knock!

Voice: Who's there?

Neighbor: I have your sock!
It was in my wash.

Painter: Knock, knock!

Voice: Who's there?

Painter: I came to borrow
a smock, Mr. Brock.

Clockmaker: Knock, knock!

Voice: Who's there?

Clockmaker: I fixed your clock, Mr. Brock.
Tick-tock!

Mail Carrier: I wish Mr. Brock
would open the door.
Other people on the block
need their mail.

25 Fun Word Family Plays © 2011 by Pamela Chanko, Scholastic Teaching Resources

Neighbor: I'll try again.
Knock, knock!

Voice: Who's there?

Painter: He's home.
I heard him.
Why won't he open the door?

Clockmaker: Maybe the lock is broken.

Mr. Brock: Hello.
What are you all doing here?

Mail Carrier: Mr. Brock!
Where did you come from?

Mr. Brock: I was on my boat.
I came from the dock.

Painter: But we heard you inside!
You answered every knock!

Mr. Brock: Ha, ha!
I see what happened.
It was my pet parrot, Sherlock!

Neighbor: What a shock!
He sounds just like you!
Did you teach him
to answer the door?

Mr. Brock: No.
He just likes
my knock-knock jokes!

The End

✦✦✦✦✦✦

25 Fun Word Family Plays © 2011 by Pamela Chanko, Scholastic Teaching Resources

Bip and Bop Shop for Pop

(At the mall)

Bip: We need to find
a gift for Pop.

Bop: We'll shop until we drop!

Bip: We can't stop at every store.
Let's go this way.

Bop: Stop!
I see a gift for Pop!
That mop will sop up spills.

Bip: Pop doesn't need a mop.
Come on, we can't stop.
We have to shop.

Bop: Stop!
I see a gift for Pop!
That knife will chop things.

Bip: Pop doesn't need to chop.
Come on, we can't stop.
We have to shop.

Bop: Stop!
I see a gift for Pop!
That bunny will hop and hop!

Bip: Pop doesn't need a bunny to hop.
He doesn't need a knife to chop!
And he doesn't need a mop to sop.
Bop, I'm tired!
I'm ready to drop!

Bop: It's okay, Bip.
We can stop.

Bip: We can't stop.
We have to shop.
I don't want Pop's gift
to be a flop!

Bop: STOP!
I see a gift for Pop!

Bip: You're right!
Pop will love it, Bop!

(At home)

Pop: It's a popcorn popper!

Bop: Turn it on!
It goes, "Pop, Pop, Pop"!

Pop: It's perfect! Thank you!

Bip: It was Bop who made me stop!

Bop: Well, I just know how
to shop for Pop!

The End

◆◆◆◆◆◆◆

25 Fun Word Family Plays © 2011 by Pamela Chanko, Scholastic Teaching Resources

Hot Dog!

Characters

Beagle	Woman
Dalmatian	Scot
Dachshund	Scot's Mom
Man	

Beagle: Arf, arf, arf!
I need a home.
I'm a cute dog with a spot.

Dalmatian: Arf, arf, arf!
I need one, too.
I'm covered with lots of dots!

Dachshund: I need a home,
but I'm long and brown,
and I don't have a spot or dots.

Beagle: You look just like a hot dog!
What chance have you got?

Dalmatian: You should learn a trick, like me.
Watch me jump over my cot!

Man: What a dog!
I'll take you home,
and I will call you Dot!

**Dachshund
and Beagle:** Hooray! You got a home!
So long and good luck, Dot!

25 Fun Word Family Plays © 2011 by Pamela Chanko, Scholastic Teaching Resources

Beagle: You should learn to run, like me.
Watch how fast I trot!

Woman: What a dog!
I'll take you home,
and I will call you Spot!

Dachshund: Hooray! You got a home!
So long and good luck, Spot!

Beagle: Learn a trick, and you'll be next.
At least it's worth a shot!

Dachshund: My legs are too short to jump or run.
This long body is all that I've got!
I'll just curl up in the corner.
I wish I were special.
But I'm not.

Scot: Look at that dog, Mom!
He can tie himself in a knot!

Scot's Mom: He looks like a hot dog!
I think we should take him, Scot.

Scot: We'll take you home and call you . . .
Hot Dog!

Dachshund: Arf!

Scot's Mom: He's saying he likes
that name a lot!

The End

25 Fun Word Family Plays © 2011 by Pamela Chanko, Scholastic Teaching Resources

Bad-Luck Chuck

Characters

Buck	Joy
Chuck	Roy

Buck: Let's all go out to play today.
Are you coming, Chuck?

Chuck: It's nice of you to ask me.
But I don't want to, Buck.

Joy: Why not?
What's the matter?

Chuck: I am sad.
I have bad luck.

Roy: I don't think that's true at all.

Buck: You're very lucky, Chuck.

Joy: You just got a new toy car.

Chuck: But I wanted to get a new truck.

Roy: What about your brand new kite?

Chuck: Look in the tree.
It's stuck.

25 Fun Word Family Plays © 2011 by Pamela Chanko, Scholastic Teaching Resources

Buck: Your team just won the hockey game.

Chuck: But then we lost the puck.

Roy: You have a nice pet chicken.

Chuck: But my chicken will not cluck.

Joy: Your apple tree is pretty.

Chuck: I don't like apples.
Yuck!

Buck: We are sorry you're unhappy.

Roy: We all care about you, Chuck.

Joy: What can we do to help you?

Buck: How can we change your luck?

Chuck: You just did!
I feel much better.
Who cares if my kite got stuck?
I have good friends,
and that makes me a lucky duck!

The End

✦ ✦ ✦ ✦ ✦ ✦

25 Fun Word Family Plays © 2011 by Pamela Chanko, Scholastic Teaching Resources

Sammy Slug Gets Snug

Sally Slug   Sonny Slug
Sandy Slug   Sammy Slug

Sally Slug: It is getting cold outside!
It's time for our winter nap.

Sandy Slug: I dug a hole for us.

Sonny Slug: I'll lug down our things.

Sally Slug: What a snug hole you dug!
Thank you, Sandy Slug.

Sandy Slug: Is everyone inside?
I will plug up the hole.

Sally Slug: Now we are snug until spring!

Sonny Slug: What's the matter, Sammy Slug?

Sammy Slug: I'm still cold.
I don't feel snug.

Sally Slug: Drink this mug of hot tea.
Is that better?

Sammy Slug: No.
I don't feel snug.

25 Fun Word Family Plays © 2011 by Pamela Chanko, Scholastic Teaching Resources

Sandy Slug: I made some yummy bug stew.
Have some from this jug.
Is that better?

Sammy Slug: No.
I don't feel snug.

Sonny Slug: Get under this rug.
Is that better?

Sammy Slug: No.
I don't feel snug.

Sally Slug: I gave you a mug of tea.

Sandy Slug: I made you a jug of stew.

Sonny Slug: I gave you a rug to get under.
But nothing we do
can make you snug!

Sammy Slug: I have an idea.
Let's try a . . .

All: . . . GROUP HUG!

**Sally,
Sandy, and
Sonny Slug:** Is that better?

Sammy Slug: Yes!
I just needed a hug!
Now I'm snug
as a slug in a rug!

The End

✦ ✦ ✦ ✦ ✦ ✦ ✦

25 Fun Word Family Plays © 2011 by Pamela Chanko, Scholastic Teaching Resources

Freddy Frump Is a Grump

Characters
Granny Frump   Travis Trump
Trudy Trump   Freddy Frump

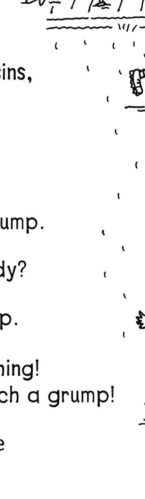

Granny: I'm Granny Frump.
My grandkids are here!
There's Freddy Frump!
He rode up with his cousins,
Travis and Trudy Trump!

Trudy: We're happy to see you,
Granny Frump!

Travis: But Freddy is being a grump.

Granny: What's the matter, Freddy?

Freddy: In the car, we hit a bump.

Trudy: Oh! That bump was nothing!
Freddy Frump, you're such a grump!

Travis: Granny Frump, watch me
play my drum!

Freddy: It's so noisy!
Thump, thump, thump!

Travis: Oh! Those thumps are nothing!
Freddy Frump, you're such a grump!

25 Fun Word Family Plays © 2011 by Pamela Chanko, Scholastic Teaching Resources

Trudy: Watch me dance
on the stump of that tree.

Freddy: Your feet go clump, clump, clump!

Trudy: Oh! Those clumps are nothing!
Freddy Frump, you're such a grump!

**Travis
and Trudy:** Bump, thump, clump!
Freddy Frump, you're such a grump!

Granny: Freddy, lie down.
You look tired.

Freddy: That mattress has a great big lump.

Granny: But the pillows are nice and plump.
You're just grumpy.
Look at how your shoulders slump.

Freddy: Well, the others are good at something.
All I'm good at is being a grump.

Granny: That's not true!
Here, try this jump rope.

Freddy: I'm good at it!
I can jump rope, Granny Frump!

**Travis
and Trudy:** Freddy Frump, you're not a grump!
Just look at you go!
Jump, Freddy, jump!

The End

✦ ✦ ✦ ✦ ✦ ✦

25 Fun Word Family Plays © 2011 by Pamela Chanko, Scholastic Teaching Resources

Mr. Crunk's Junk

-unk

Characters

Gary Grunk   Mr. Crunk
Mrs. Crunk

Gary Grunk: My name is Gary Grunk.
I live next door to Mr. Crunk.
He had lots and lots of junk.
Until one day, when Mrs. Crunk
smelled something.
It stunk!

Mrs. Crunk: What is that funk?
I'm throwing out the junk.

Mr. Crunk: No, Mrs. Crunk!

Mrs. Crunk: This tub has a missing chunk.

Mr. Crunk: So? It's still good for a dunk!

Gary Grunk: But it was junk to Mrs. Crunk.
It went in the trash.
Ker-plunk!

Mrs. Crunk: These boots are covered with gunk.

Mr. Crunk: So? I like the way they clunk!

25 Fun Word Family Plays © 2011 by Pamela Chanko, Scholastic Teaching Resources

Gary Grunk: But they were junk to Mrs. Crunk.
They went in the trash.
Ker-plunk!

Mrs. Crunk: This sweater must have shrunk.

Mr. Crunk: So? I like it!
It's got spunk!

Gary Grunk: But it was junk to Mrs. Crunk.
It went in the trash.
Ker-plunk!

Mr. Crunk: All that's left is that old trunk!
Let me keep it, Mrs. Crunk.

Mrs. Crunk: Okay. We'll keep the trunk.
But I still smell that funk!
What can it be?
We threw out all the junk!

Mr. Crunk: Did you just hear a thunk?

Mrs. Crunk: Should we open up the trunk?

**Mr. and
Mrs. Crunk:** YIKES!

Mr. Crunk: Something was inside that trunk . . .

Mrs. Crunk: . . . and it's running
to the home of Gary Grunk!

25 Fun Word Family Plays © 2011 by Pamela Chanko, Scholastic Teaching Resources

**Mr. and
Mrs. Crunk:** Whatever was in there stunk!

Gary Grunk: And this ends the story
of Mr. Crunk's junk:
On the day that the Crunks
threw away all the junk,
they also found Skippy—
my long lost pet skunk!

The End

25 Fun Word Family Plays © 2011 by Pamela Chanko, Scholastic Teaching Resources